JAN 2011

Louisiana

BY AMY VAN ZEE

The Child's World

Published by The Child's World®
1980 Lookout Drive • Mankato, MN 56003-1705
800-599-READ • www.childsworld.com

ACKNOWLEDGMENTS
The Child's World®: Mary Berendes, Publishing Director
The Design Lab: Design and production
Red Line Editorial: Editorial direction

PHOTO CREDITS: Ken Durden/Shutterstock Images, cover, 1, 3; Matt Kania/
Map Hero, Inc., 4, 5; Vikrant Azad/iStockphoto, 7; Darryl Lodato/iStockphoto,
9; Louis Bourgeois/Shutterstock, 10; Kristine Carrier/iStockphoto, 11; Bill
Haber/AP Images, 13; North Wind Picture Archives/Photolibrary, 15; EauClaire
Media/iStockphoto, 17; AP Images, 19; Jason Major/iStockphoto, 21; One
Mile Up, 22; Quarter-dollar coin image from the United States Mint, 22

LIBRARY OF CONGRESS CATALOGING-IN-PUBLICATION DATA
Van Zee, Amy.
  Louisiana / by Amy Van Zee.
      p. cm.
  Includes bibliographical references and index.
  ISBN 978-1-60253-462-9 (library bound : alk. paper)
  1. Louisiana—Juvenile literature. I. Title.

F369.3.V36 2010
976.3—dc22

                    2010017714

Printed in the United States of America in Mankato, Minnesota.
July 2010
F11538

On the cover:
Pirates Alley is a
street in the French
Quarter area of
New Orleans,
Louisiana.

CONTENTS

Geography

Let's explore Louisiana! Louisiana is in the southern United States. The **Gulf** of Mexico is to the south of Louisiana.

ARKANSAS

Oil City

Shreveport

Lake Bistineau

Monroe

Epps

MISSISSIPPI

Mississippi River

LOUISIANA

TEXAS

Natchitoches

Bermuda

NORTH
WEST
EAST
SOUTH

Alexandria

Opelousas

Baton Rouge

Lake Charles

Lafayette

Vacherie

Lake Pontchartrain

New Iberia

New Orleans

Houma

Gulf of Mexico

Cities

Baton Rouge is the capital of Louisiana. New Orleans is the largest city in the state. Shreveport and Lafayette are other large cities.

New Orleans is located along the Mississippi River. ▶

Land

The Mississippi River flows through Louisiana and empties into the Gulf of Mexico. Louisiana has rolling hills, **prairies**, **marshes**, and **bayous**. A bayou is a swampy and slow-moving body of water.

Many of Louisiana's marshes are close to the coast. ▶

Lake Pontchartrain is Louisiana's largest lake. It is 40 miles (64 km) long!

Plants and Animals

About 40 percent of Louisiana is wetland. The bald cypress is the state tree. Louisiana's state bird is the brown pelican. This bird has a large bill with a pouch in it. The flower of the magnolia tree is the state flower. Magnolia trees are found throughout the state.

These bald cypress trees grow in Lake Bistineau, Louisiana. ▶

11

People and Work

Almost 4.5 million people live in Louisiana. Many people work in jobs that help **tourists**. Other people work in **manufacturing**, mining, or farming.

Cotton and sugarcane are crops grown in Louisiana. Shrimp and fish are also caught off its coast and then sold.

Some people in Louisiana grow strawberries. ▶

PRODUCT OF U.S.A.

12
1 PINT

A PRODUCT OF
CERTIFIED
LOUISIANA

12
1 PINT

PRODUCT OF U.S.A.

12
1 PINT

A PRODUCT OF
CERTIFIED
LOUISIANA

PRODUCT OF U.S.A.

PRODUCT OF U.S.A.

PRODUCT OF U.S.A.

A PRODUCT OF
CERTIFIED

12

12

12

1 PINT

History

Native Americans have lived in the Louisiana area for thousands of years. Spain first ruled the Louisiana area in the 1500s. Its location at the end of the Mississippi River made it valuable for trade. France and England later ruled the area. U.S. President Thomas Jefferson bought the land from France in 1803. Louisiana became the eighteenth state on April 30, 1812.

The Louisiana Purchase in 1803 made the United States much larger. Although it was named after the state, ▶ the area included much more land than Louisiana.

Ways of Life

Mardi Gras is a famous **festival** in Louisiana. People from many places travel to New Orleans for Mardi Gras. They wear colorful clothing and masks and watch **parades**. **Jazz** is enjoyed in Louisiana. People in Louisiana visit **museums**. Some people like to hunt and fish, too.

People dress in costumes and pass out ▶ necklaces at Mardi Gras parades.

Famous People

Jazz musician Louis Armstrong was born in Louisiana. He played the trumpet and sang. Writer Truman Capote was from Louisiana. Many of his stories take place in the South. Peyton and Eli Manning grew up in Louisiana. They are both quarterbacks in the National Football League.

Louis Armstrong (center) became famous in the 1920s. ▶

Famous Places

Many people travel to Louisiana to visit the French Quarter in New Orleans. This area of the city contains many old buildings. Louisiana also has many **plantations**. Plantations are large farms where crops are grown. Many were built before the U.S. **Civil War**. Visitors can tour these large homes and farms.

Many people visit Oak Alley Plantation in Vacherie, Louisiana. ▶

State Symbols

Seal

Louisiana's state seal shows an adult pelican feeding its young. Go to childsworld.com/links for a link to Louisiana's state Web site, where you can get a firsthand look at the state seal.

Flag

The state flag has the state seal on it. On the flag is the state's **motto**, "Union, Justice & Confidence."

Quarter

A pelican and a trumpet are on the Louisiana state quarter. The quarter came out in 2002.

Glossary

bayous (BYE-ooz): Bayous are swampy and slow-moving bodies of water. Louisiana has many bayous.

Civil War (SIV-il WOR): In the United States, the Civil War was a war fought between the Northern and the Southern states from 1861 to 1865. Many of Louisiana's large houses were built before the Civil War.

festival (FESS-tih-vul): A festival is a celebration for an event or holiday. Mardi Gras is a famous festival in New Orleans.

gulf (GULF): A gulf is a large body of water with land around most of it. Louisiana is along the Gulf of Mexico.

jazz (JAZ): Jazz is a type of music where musicians add notes in unexpected places. Jazz is popular in Louisiana.

manufacturing (man-yuh-FAK-chur-ing): Manufacturing is the task of making items with machines. Some people in Louisiana work in manufacturing.

marshes (MARSH-ez): Marshes are wet, low lands. Louisiana has marshes.

motto (MOT-oh): A motto is a sentence that states what people stand for or believe. Louisiana's motto is "Union, Justice & Confidence."

museums (myoo-ZEE-umz): Museums are places where people go to see art, history, or science displays. People in Louisiana visit museums.

parades (puh-RAYDZ): Parades are when people march to honor holidays. There are Mardi Gras parades in Louisiana.

plantations (plan-TAY-shunz): Plantations are large farms where crops are grown. Louisiana has many old plantations.

prairies (PRAYR-eez): Prairies are flat or hilly grasslands. Louisiana has prairies.

seal (SEEL): A seal is a symbol a state uses for government business. A pelican is on the Louisiana seal.

sugarcane (SHUG-ur-kayn): Sugarcane is a tall grass with sugar in its stem. Sugarcane is grown in Louisiana.

symbols (SIM-bulz): Symbols are pictures or things that stand for something else. The seal and flag are Louisiana's symbols.

tourists (TOOR-ists): Tourists are people who visit a place (such as a state or country) for fun. Tourists come to Louisiana for its festivals and history.

Further Information

Books

Downing, Johnette. *Down in Louisiana: Traditional Song*. Gretna, LA: Pelican Publishing Company, 2007.

Prieto, Anita. *P is for Pelican: A Louisiana Alphabet*. Chelsea, MI: Sleeping Bear Press, 2004.

Reynolds, Jeff. *A to Z: United States of America*. New York: Children's Press, 2004.

Web Sites

Visit our Web site for links about Louisiana: *childsworld.com/links*

Note to Parents, Teachers, and Librarians: We routinely verify our Web links to make sure they are safe and active sites. So encourage your readers to check them out!

Index